ALL ABOUT TRAFFIC

How to Beat
A Parking Summons

Traffic Platoon Commander

authorHOUSE®

AuthorHouse™
1663 Liberty Drive
Bloomington, IN 47403
www.authorhouse.com
Phone: 1 (800) 839-8640

Published by AuthorHouse   03/31/2016

ISBN: 978-1-5049-8146-0 (sc)
ISBN: 978-1-5049-8145-3 (e)

Print information available on the last page.

Any people depicted in stock imagery provided by Thinkstock are models, and such images are being used for illustrative purposes only.
Certain stock imagery © Thinkstock.

This book is printed on acid-free paper.

ALL ABOUT TRAFFIC
&
HOW TO BEAT A PARKING SUMMONS

By (RETIRED) Traffic Supervisor II
Gary Bromberg

Just so everybody is aware I suffered from a stroke and a seizure on August 2, 2014 and I do believe I did keep my records up to date. Most of my days are not be the same in any shape or form because many times now my memory comes and goes a lot and it goes all due to one(1) him or her, person. I do get very depressed from all of this. Many days my head is in a daze that is hard to get it out because all I want to do is get revenge on that person because I don't deserve how I feel. Why did I have a stroke and a seizure, it was all from stress which only he or she caused it all for me. I started working for the Department of Transportation Bureau of Traffic Enforcement on August. 2. 1982 in Long Island City to become a Traffic Enforcement Agent. I worked till January 2014 and I was legally forced to retire with a transfer with a bunch of lies from that person who does work for Traffic Enforcement which was on Jan. 27. 2014. That was my last day because I had to use up all my time. Unfortunately, the Police Department is very corrupt. A Traffic Supervisor calls the other Traffic Supervisors to question him or her about certain things and if they can't answer, then the questions they are now asking are now cancelled. The Traffic Manager doesn't have to answer anything, and that Traffic Manager now wins. This is how they win, corruption.

I was taken off all my heavy duty details which were done at night time, which was done on overtime, towing strictly heavy duty vehicles to a tow pound usually in that borough were tractor trailers, detached trailers, trucks, busses, etc. I had keys that I had found all over and they did work, especially for hard to do Volvo's with these special keys, my keys mostly started them and it was great that my keys would be able to do that to Volvo's or even Internationals or Kenworth, etc., my keys would be able to open the doors and start these tractor trailers up so they would build up air pressure, (for those who have a C.D.L. you know what I'm talking about) that detail worked so great it was unbelievable till that Traffic Manager screwed me up big time.

Now my two (2) tours are complaining because when I was working I would always find tows even if they couldn't find anything I would call their Supervisors to call their trucks to pick up these tows, and it worked out again till that Traffic Manager screwed it up good. I was even told by the Inspector of the Police Department to call in tows, but that stopped. I mean if it was big enough to tow, it was, and then I had to use up all my time because I was now being forced to retire. I was an experience Heavy Duty Towing Supervisor. I was asked to do these heavy duty details as per the Traffic Manager-2 as per then Deputy Inspector now Inspector of the Police Department because of my Heavy Duty Experience.

Then I was now transferred to Queens North, so now I was now not making any money at all, so it now costing me money to go to work, all thanks to that particular person. I was then put on a tour that had no money for me to make. I wasn't given any room at all for my paperwork or anything all because of this particular Traffic Manager-1 who is very disturbed with mental issues. I wasn't making any night shift differential, no more overtime, nothing at all. I had to deal with a lot of crap. That particular person was also a big fragrant liar who lied about everything and continues to lie, to save himself or herself.

From what I did get is the Deputy Director of Traffic knows about him or her cursing me out publicly and she denied it.

From what I got I did hear that person ordered for me not to get any overtime or night shift, nothing. What I did see and hear was I was making more money than this particular person.

Now I see since I was forced to retire, and that particular person has Traffic Supevisors-1's do the work and if they can get one (1) tow per tow truck operator it's a lot to where when I did them we were towing a lot more than one (1) tow, maybe six (6) tow per night with tow(2) trucks.

I did have at one(1) time a Supervisor a Traffic Supervisor-1 work with me and it did work out great till I was told no more because I was putting on too much overtime for nothing so I told that Supervisor and he didn't like it but he agreed to with it. There were two (2) Traffic Supervisors and the other had no idea what was actually going on because if he did any of the details he never showed up at the precincts to let them know he was there so he just hanged around outside till one (1) Sergeant questioned him and that's when it hit he was there for over two (2) hours and he never said one (1) word as to why he was there. I would have never worked like that, I would always let the desk Sergeant know I was there and I would wait outside if I wasn't comfortable inside.

Since now the heavy duty details do have a tow truck driver for towing, but not really for towing, the Manhattan Tow Pound is strictly using boots, because no tow truck driver are willing to do any heavy duty towing, but they do have a tow truck just in case of a tow. I did work my way up the ranks to Lieutenant or Traffic Supervisor-1, Captain or actually Traffic Supervisor-2 or to Platoon Commander, to which I got the respect I wanted. Although many people think differently.

Just so you are aware much of my career was in towing, I enjoyed working on cars because I was working in a repair shop before I came to Traffic, so I kept it in Traffic. I spent a lot of time then by calling in tows to help out the drivers who couldn't find any tows, I got into towing from I believe April of 1986 or so, then I became a Supervisor in 1990 and then Captain till 2001 or around there.

What everybody wants to know about Traffic, or thinks they know, and don't. What everybody does know within the Police Department with Police Officers there is a blue wall of silence, although mostly denied, it's there. When something happens to a cop, then you're in it for that cop or that person. Whereas within Traffic Enforcement there are more 2 legged rats than 4 legged rats, meaning your own people will rat you out in a heartbeat, if not faster regardless if you know them, or even if you don't. Within Traffic Enforcement it is a minority division and always has been, with 90% Blacks & Spanish, now 5% Indian as well Muslim and growing fast, 5 % Caucasian.

Training to be a Traffic Enforcement Agent takes approximately ten (10) weeks, learning about the Supervisor's levels, uniforms, summonses, violations, etc. Being a Traffic Enforcement Agent you have different levels of Supervisors besides Police Supervisors who are also our Supervisors, all within the Police Department. Being with the Traffic Division you must have your Driver's License, no permits or License Identifications Cards at all.

One(1) issue I did realize is cooping, cooping is when you have three (3) Traffic Agents all sitting in a restaurant or a diner eating there meals when more Traffic Agents come walking into the same restaurant or diner to eat. In Traffic Enforcement you're only permitted to have just three (3) Traffic Enforcement Agents in one (1) establishment to eat, all at the same time or you can be receiving a command discipline or you will chase out with a warning.

Today going from a level-1 Traffic Enforcement Agents to a level-3 Traffic Enforcement Agents will never happen because the union agreed that anybody in Traffic must come up the ranks, you must go up two (2) years to each of the ranks to become a level-3 Traffic Enforcement Agents-3 you must go to be a Traffic Enforcement Agent-1 meaning you must become a level-1, within two (2) years then level-2. Many Traffic Agents think you must go to a level-2 office when you don't. You can always learn it from a level-1 office and be used as a level-2 when you're needed to do level-2 work so you will be issuing summonses as your needed, when or if you become a level-3 will be taking you a towing command if you pass that test, which can be difficult.

There are different levels of Traffic Enforcement Agents because each level does something different or more than the other. A Traffic Enforcement Agent-1 issues just parking summonses, which should be phased out and used more as a level-2, Traffic Enforcement Agent-2 and used to issue moving violations as well parking summonses, a Traffic Enforcement Agenl-3 tows illegally parked vehicles as well issues parking summonses and directs direct as well used to issue moving violations, Traffic Enforcement Agent-4 goes to constructions sites and issues summonses for violations for violations being committed at constructions sites as well moving violations and parking summonses as needed and do have Special Patrolman Status as well many Supervisors have Special patrolman Status since being an agent prior to making Supervisor.

When you join Traffic Enforcement you must work mostly all the holidays, including religious holidays as long as you have time you can use, meaning annual leave, overtime owed, if your permitted to. If you do call in sick leave you had better have your documentation or you will may have a Command Discipline for being out if it's not documented.

If you do call in sick leave you can call in sick leave, but not undocumented it, you do get after a while a command discipline if you're out somewhere around eight (8) times altogether. The issue is if you're religious you can get all of them if you know what you're doing. If you're a religious Catholic and you have a letter from your Priest saying this, you may get it, same as being Jewish, you can get all the holidays if you know how do it also. There is a form called a twenty eight (28) it's for taking any time off and it's in writing that you're requesting to get your time off.

If your just starting don't expect any time off, expect to work it for at least one (1) year, if that's what your probation is, I say that because it has changed. If you're on probation, finish it before taking off unless you're really very religious with proof, then get your proof and submit a copy of it to your Supervisor, don't give that Supervisor the original unless you must, get yourself a copy and then give in the original.

When you get into Traffic Enforcement you can go up the ranks within Traffic Enforcement if you want to, you can go up to Traffic Enforcement-4 or to Traffic Supervisor- 3 or X.O. (Executive Officer) depending on you. If you went to towing and it can take you up or about three (3) month to go thru the training and that's if you pass Traffics Enforcement Towing training classes. If you don't pass the training you will be sent back to your former command and then you can reapply for training if you really want it. It basically depends on how bad you're needed at towing. If your pregnant you can start off if they allow you because if your pregnant why start off and waist everybody time learning towing. You must learn a lot to start off, first (1) off with their paper work, vouchering, vouching property, claims, field inspection book, filling out your field patrols (210) these are just some of your paper work. You must go out and buy a tow trucks operators uniform and then you start off towing, this doesn't mean you're in, yet.

This is just your uniform. You must learn all about your tow trucks, passing the test for tow truck operator endorsement all within the Department of Motor Vehicles the part of your paper work, how to tow period.

Towing takes time to learn, but you can be if you're that interested. A lot of tow truck operators can't reverse their trucks with a tow on them but it takes time, practice helps out a lot if you do it with your trainer. If you do get into towing be prepared to work all the major holidays which includes New Years, any or all major holidays regardless you will be assigned to work them and if you call in sick leave expect to have your sick note to document your time off or you will be sent back to your old command.

Towing is no joke when you're towing in somebody's vehicles you must use the department's tow straps, tow chains, rope for rear towing a vehicle which includes front wheel drive vehicles, you may have to rear tow it and you must have an idea where to look for the linkage. If you just tow in just whatever you can find without using the departments equipment then you looking for trouble as well lawsuits, which means if you're just going to just hook up the vehicle, no chains, straps, no rope for rear towing that vehicle then you may as well quit towing and go back to summons writing.

This is also for documentation you're planning on sending it in with your parking tickets, make copies, take pictures showing proof send them out and in my opinion don't expect anything special to happen, again, I would suggest you go to Parking Violations in person, argue your case and see what the Administration Law Judge decided to tell you.

If you just mail in your parking summons don't expect much to happen because when you're mailing your summons the Administration Law Judge can just send it back to you saying you're guilty or maybe if you send it to him the correct way you may win your case. I'm saying it this way because many people are just plain to lazy, and they want to see what will happen. I would suggest if you can make a copy of your summons, your registration showing the problem, if that or pictures to show your right.

The Administration Law Judge has to do it the right way and say you're not guilty or he or she just may lower your fine, but you're still guilty. I always suggest going to the Parking Violations Bureau because if it done right, you should be a winner.

Whoever starts off as a Traffic Agent must sign in before doing anything, the sign in book is at the front desk or actually outside by the front desk, you must sign in for the Traffic Supervisor can see who is in and who is out or even late. Then when you sign in you must go to your locker room and get dressed and wait for your assignment. There are two (2) books that sit by the front desk one (1) of them is called the front desk log book and the other book is called the telephone log book, which book must be logged in so now the Desk Supervisor can see who called out for that day, either sick leave, e-day, annual leave, or whatever they called in which includes emergency leave, sick leave, death in your family, etc.. Whatever the case is you must call in. If you're the desk Supervisor you must log in who, and why they are calling, the time they did call and why they called in, if you don't then you can expect a Command Discipline coming your way.

The reasons I'm explaining this is because whoever you are must show the whereabouts for that person if they don't show up for work on that day, which includes tour changes, they must be called in or denied. At the Manhattan Tow Pound there are always Traffic Agents that do call in but the desk Supervisor either fails to log it forget to log it because he or she is always on their cell phone which is illegal.

Many people do call and the front desk Supervisor gets so busy he forgets but writes it down because when you log that you must also log your roll call explaining what you spoke about for that particular day, which does includes no hits or whatever you spoke about for that day, it can include volunteers for that day to respond to a funeral for that day or future days. All this information is necessary to be logged.

All agents must start with their tours by fifteen minutes past the hour, so if their tours starts at 1: 00 P.M. they must be ready by 1:15 even if their immediate Supervisors aren't ready, they must be, in regards to roll call, every Traffic Agents must be prepared to hear about or do anything about anything, no hits, closers, whatever must be spoken to about their immediate supervisor or higher, which does include funerals for a M.O.S., which is called upon. Then at the end of your tour it must be the minute you can sign out for, not one (1) minute before or else you can be written up or command discipline.

When their roll call starts they should be ready, or you can be put in the minor violation book, which hardly happened, because usually a higher rank wanted to speak with that particular Agent so they were speaking with he or she, then stand at attention, be in complete uniform for that day and if their immediate supervisors call for rain coats are the order for that day, the agents may have to go back to their lockers even if the day appears to be nice, they must go back and get their rain coats. All Traffic Agents must also carry vests as it became the law that if writing any summonses they must be visible at all times. If your motorized you still must wear your vest or have your rain coat in case if rain.

Whatever your orders are for that day are to be followed, no excuses, or else a Command Discipline can or will be followed to its fullest.

All Command are completely different although it varies in different ways. The Police Department does have Captains throughout the department, each command has a different way of doing their own ways and it must be kept up or you will be facing command disciplines. The Chief Of Transportation has a Duty Captain and his way is to be traveling the City of New York and patrol the City no matter where the issue is he is that Captain and he can make up his mind to issues that may need a quick call to be made up, if he isn't sure, he can call his Deputy Inspector or higher and get a quick decision, either way it does get done, and correctly.

If you do get a parking ticket for a meter, the best thing you can do is if you can find the person who wrote the summons and ask him or her if he can try to dismiss the summons, that's if the summons is five (5) minutes or less he or she can dismiss the summons, if it more than five (5) minutes, he can't. If that Traffic Agent is in the middle of writing a summons you must wait for that Traffic Agent to finish that summons don't try to be forceful or threaten that Traffic Agents because today many are new Traffic Agents and many new Traffic Agents are used to dismissing that summons and calling for their Supervisor is going to take more time unless their Supervisor is standing right there, then it's questionable if it can be done at all.

If that person is writing somebody a summons to somebody else immediately you can't expect them to take your back no matter how long your waiting it's yours, that's your summons, it's the law now that if a Traffic Agent writes a parking summons for a parking meter it can be dismissed if you can find the Traffic Agent who wrote that summons. Don't start cursing that Traffic Agent because he is doing just his job, because he can't help you if the summons is too old, more than Five (5) minutes.

Within Traffic we do have a Director of the Parking Enforcement District which started as an Traffic Enforcement Agent to Lieutenant, then he made Captain, then he got to Inspector, then he made Chief, then he got to Chief of a higher rank and is now in charge of by being called the Director Of Traffic within Traffic Division, specialty in towing, but has the control of all Traffic Division, with the Inspector of the Police Department who does assist him in his own ways, who issues memo's and in police terms are called forty nines "49's" which are written daily giving instructions or advising daily about details coming down in the future, or advising instructions to be followed, as well as such as closing down streets for block party's', street fairs, president in town, marathons, etc.

Many of these 49's have the person's name on the top and bottom stating who it is from and many can be from the Commanding Officer but if the name is not signed on the bottom the excuse can be that person didn't write it or it can be sign by somebody else for that person as long as it is signed, but if not followed you may be getting a Command Discipline for not following that 49 although not signed because it maybe not be a lawful order, which is very common within the Police Department. Many orders are not lawful but are expected to be followed.

For a few years now a Traffic Agent have been a level-2 since graduating the academy because there are emergencies that arise at any time and a Traffic Agent is required to direct Traffic at a moment's notice in all kinds of weather. As for Supervisors in D.O.T we started out as Lieutenants as 1 St line supervisors, no Sergeant's, then came Captains, then Inspectors, then Chief, who was in charge of a command, then another Chief of a higher rank who was in charge of all commands, meaning for example towing.

A Chief would be charge of the Bronx tow pound, another for Queens Tow pound, another for Brooklyn tow pound, another for Manhattan pound. Then the big Chief for all Tow pounds, same goes for Enforcement, which is summons writing, which are now called Traffic Managers.

What everybody talks about is a quota, how many summonses must a Traffic Agent write? The term used in Traffic is really an office average, as well squad average, which is the same as a quota. What it really means is how many summonses one Traffic Agent must write or tow or do on a daily basis. Each summons command or tow pound has a number they must meet on a daily basis to make their monthly number as well there yearly number.

Not in towing because there summons count is just for summons writing commands, not for towing, they get there tow count to where it should be and then that tow operator is doing great. If they don't make that number they are below average.

Office of Management and Budget (O.M.B.) tells the city how many summonses or tows they must do each month as well the year in order to get extra money for cars, or supplies, etc. For their commands to operate properly or keep what they have if they don't make that number. I do know that is a lot of things I could probably be talking about, but right now I can't remember them.

What many people don't know is that the end of the fiscal year which is the last day in June, beginning of July. 1st is the beginning of the new fiscal year if that command makes there number of summonses or tows that Traffic Manager gets a raise which is really not spoken about, but it happens.

Some Traffic Managers will make a party around the fourth of July for their Traffic Agents out of appreciation for the hard work they do day in and day out, whereas many managers don't consider being that July 1st is the beginning of the new fiscal year.

A motorized Traffic agent is required to write approximately forty tow (42) or so summonses daily as a passenger or foot patrol agent is required to write approximately twenty seven (27) or so summonses daily as a tow operator is required to tow at least three (3) vehicles daily whereas a heavy duty operator is required to tow two (2) tows daily. All Traffic Agents used to be required to carry 75 paper summonses which were switched over to computerize summonses with a P.T.D. (Parking Ticket Device) as well that printer to print the parking summons which must be carried. Here is the main question n everybody wants to know, how do I beat the summons? What I would suggest doing is this, go to the parking violations bureau and see the Admiration Law Judge in person, argue your point, bring pictures to show him or her and then you may have a case, just mailing the summons out in the mail, you lose because the Admiration Law Judge has nobody there to argue, so you lose, he can just send the summons back saying, you're, your guilty.

I always saw this is, the higher you write the more the higher ups want, meaning if you can write twenty five (25) they want thirty (30) or better, or else. Agents can only write what they see or they will get written up for writing somewhat less start writing bogus summonses to make their count seem higher, not all of them, but a few might or they may even write a motorist a summons who said something wrong to them so they kept they kept their plate number so they always write them even with their vin #.

Like issuing a summons to a car that is half way in a no parking anytime sign, they may write it to get that higher number, I've seen it as well most of the police officers will, just to get that higher number of summonses.

Now to come D.C.P.I. which is the Deputy Commissioner Public Information (646-610-6700) which usually happened when something happens all within the Police Department, or when something happen all within Traffic or even with School Safety. Anything can happen and we are never permitted to speak, only the D.C.P.I does. It's about whenever the situation happens. Like when that Traffic Agent got run over by a heavy duty truck in Midtown Manhattan, only D.C.P.I got the agents information, gave all the information correctly to the Police Commissioner, and he read their words to everybody, from who, his was, age, family, etc.

What I do see is that Traffic Enforcement Agents or higher never get to say one(1) word even if they know what it is they are saying, they can't say it or face a command discipline, whereas a Police Officer can speak and he'll never get a command discipline.

Many times they won't speak until he or she situation can be verified completely. Even the press channels can't talk to Traffic Enforcement without D.C.P.I getting involved in there talking.

An issue I see is the Citywide Bikes, they are allowed to be parked in a violation, meaning No standing. If cars were never allowed to be parked there how can these bikes be allowed to sit there and do nothing. I find it bad enough that these bikes are cluttering up the city streets because who would want to ride a bike in Midtown Manhattan when it's not safe.

How commercial stores get there deliveries when you have these bikes being parked there. What I do realized is the former mayors son in-law got there contract for city bikes.

One (1) of the issues I now have are the people I used to work with, many of these people are good people to whereas many of them today aren't as good as they used to be, many of these people became very lazy, worn out, tired, etc. The newer people are still good people although not as experienced as the experienced people once were.

A problem I found out is that many older and newer experienced tow operators get caught doing illegal things, like stealing. If that person gets caught, they can get fired or even suspended or receive a Command Discipline. Either way who wants it?

As it stands many vehicles have been down for the longest because they are not fixed properly because the Police Department feels they need our cars so they take them, like we don't know what really happened. Today in the Police Department their cars have their writing done on their hoods saying Police Department. Then under that it can say Traffic Enforcement, School Safety, and Police Department. Or have it changed to just the Police Department, so anyway you look into it they get what they wanted.

The Manhattan Tow Pound has Shop # 8 which is a major part of the tow pound. This shop also takes care of much of the Police Department not all but with maybe eight (8) mechanics, but then there are also other Shops all around this city. This shop works on small tow trucks, as well many different types of cars throughout the city but the last I remember there is one(1) mechanic who can work on heavy duty tow trucks but not anymore because he don't get paid for it so now he refuses to.

Within the city, the city has contracts to fix flat tires so you don't have to wait to get to long to get your tires fixed and all you have to do is found out where these contractors fix tires, many of these contractors are not too far from your command.

The situation is that the Manhattan Tow Pound is the main tow pound, we were told about brand new trucks and when we got one (1) or two (2) of them, they had to be sent back to the dealer because what we got was tow (2) wheel drive, meaning just the rear wheels were the drive wheels, are now getting these all-wheel drive, new trucks slowly. That was in 2012 and now we are starting to get the new trucks.

The new trucks were supposed to be at all the tow pound by July and they finally started showed up, one (1) at a time, going to the highest tow operators 1 St, then as they come in then everybody will have a new truck. The issue is when we do get these new tow trucks only a few people will be taking care these trucks, because if a tow truck goes down for whatever reasons they never check out the trucks for anything leaving that truck down for ever or it may have to go back to the dealer for repairs. The reason for these new trucks is because if there is an emergency we must arrive or show up with everything the Police are required to carry with them and possibly more. The issues is we have never been trained for this and where is the money we are supposed to be receiving for doing this.

Now I see and hear that the city bought new Smart cars, just enough seating room for 1 just person and I found that to be very dangerous especially used in Manhattan because the size of the vehicle, and other reasons that can hurt the driver(s) because the city took away their scooters and they gave them Smart cars. I guess for each its own.

The Police Department is appreciated to a point, but when it comes to writing summonses, they can make mistakes as well, and get away with it. Some Police Officers do know how to write a parking summonses and the newly promoted Police Officers who was at one (1) time Traffic Agents, they can write whatever to be needed, no problems.

Any lost Police Department equipment must be reported to the local precinct regardless if it's a P.T.D. which is really called Parking Ticket Device or radio, or keys, ID card, shield, anything, etc. where that agent will receive a command discipline for failure to safeguard Police Department property, even if found the command discipline will stand as long as a number has been generated for that complaint by the precinct, which is called a 61 that agent will be receiving a command discipline. Don't let any supervisor try to fool you by saying it's done already because in many cases it isn't unless his or hers supervisor tell you differently. If you spent all day trying to locate that property and you finally found it, then you can expect to hear about that Command Discipline.

Each roll of summonses for a P.T.D. is now 100 in a roll and all agents must carry a new roll and some tow operators will carry paper summonses and envelopes. If a P.T.D. freezes up or won't work properly there Supervisor must respond to that agent with another P.T.D. for them to use as well battery's.

If a summons is in the P.T.D. and is stuck in it that summons cannot be voided but may be sent in a refusal summons, which means if your waiting patiently for your summons or for the supervisor to respond, you will get that summons whereas if you leave, you will most likely get that summons in your mail costing you at least an extra $15 dollars or so or even more. Reason being for the P.T.D. is because Administrative law judges could not always understand or read what the summons said so it had to be dismissed and now if the agent doesn't check the summons because the P.T.D. can make errors, which it does, then that summons can be dismissed.

No Traffic Agents are permitted to bring a summons back to the command because he or she made an error, a supervisor must respond to that agent's location to verify the problem to void that summons; it can be an integrity issue. Police Officers do carry the old paper summons and do make many errors and can be dismissed only if you know what the mistake is.

There are several types. If a summons is altered it is now an invalid summons which should not be issued and most are, or face being written up if you're caught. If anybody makes an error on the summons then they are required to stop at that point and begin a new summons and void out the error summons. If it becomes an issue where an agent is not writing what's required everyday then that immediate supervisor is required to sit with that agent and write a conferral showing they spoke with that agent to find out why they are not writing what they are required to write, which also goes for tow operators, a level-2 Traffic agent is not required to write summonses unless needed because keeping traffic flowing during rush hours is there priority's, not issuing summonses, but are as required to keep traffic flowing free and smooth as well calling for a department tow truck to remove the vehicles causing his or her intersection from flowing freely. This is why a summons is needed otherwise no summonses are written.

There are many contradicting issues within the Police Department which writing a conferral is an example, it is a made up memo within the Police Department which we were all told if you only spoke to that person, then you did nothing to fix the problem, whereas if you wrote up a conferral, you sign it and not the person you supposedly spoke to means you did something to fix that error. A conferral can be written at any time but the agents name can be on it without them even knowing about it, that's wrong, but is it done.

While we were in Department of Transportation Traffic agents were called Brownie's because we all wore brown uniforms or called meter maids as we are still called because the main function was to write summonses were expired meters as well tow illegally parked vehicles regardless of size, which can also and does mean from cars, motorcycles, vans, trucks, buses, tractor trailers, detached trailers, etc.

While in D.O.T. we had many assaults in which the police were called in to make the arrest and that lead to issues because many times the police either didn't show up or it took hours for them to respond and the motorist always got off with a slap on the wrist with a fine of maybe $50 or so compared to today where the perp will be arrested no matter what, no desk appearance ticket no matter who says so. Back then the perp would be arrested and depending on if department property was damaged the perp would have to pay for the damage and if the agent was hurt the charges would go up. Reasons were because while in D.O.T. Traffic Agents were ordered to issue summonses to police officers personal cars for Quality of Life violations even with restricted parking permits in the windows and as their way of retaliating if a Traffic Agent was assaulted they took their time responding. Today if you assault Traffic Agent it's a whole different story altogether. No desk appearance ticket, mainly jail time only.

If that person don't get any jail time then it becomes a bigger problem to where the Inspector will set that cop straight by telling them they must be arrested and booked.

When we merged into the Police Department in 1996 all our uniforms were then changed to navy blue which was the old colors of the Police Officers because the police officers all wore navy blue so we are wearing their old uniforms making all of us look like police officers, whereas now Police Officers now wear black except for higher rank supervisors who wear a white shirt above Sargent.

As it is we are no longer permitted to write any summonses to any type of parking permits regardless if expired Police Department or Handicap permit although a handicap permit can be issued a parking summons but not towed because nobody can say what the disability is of the handicap permit although I have seen many drivers in a bus stop with the bus there unloading passengers getting a summons running out of the store saying how they were only there for two seconds as those are the orders that came down and explained to us why would you want to write up another member of service when you don't know what they are doing which can mean using their personal vehicle for department business or it can be a unmarked department vehicle with expired registration and inspection stickers, an agent should be able to recognize it with the orange EZ pass on the window as a department vehicle and not issue any summonses.

If that Police Department Office or a higher rank is parked where he or she is not permitted they must put in there Department Parking permit or how would anybody know whose car it really belongs to.

We are still referred to as meter maids or brownies because of the public's ignorance because now Traffic Agents of all ranks do a lot more now as far as enforcement goes than years ago.

As it is nobody is permitted to be allowed to try to fix their own vehicle on a highway or bridge do to the very congestion traffic being all around them no matter if in the middle of the night or during the day, it's a law that you can't fix your car on a highway or bridge also many people do try it anyway, they can either drive off the highway or bridge or have an authorized tow truck removes them, those are the rules.

The Police Department also has a help program for those who may break down on a major highway or a bridge they assist them or call for authorized tow as needed. Our prior mayor had this idea of having a tablet installed in every (Radio Motorized Patrol) R.M.P. as well department tow truck as well the supervisors vehicles because when a illegally parked vehicle regardless of what kind of vehicle from a car, motorcycle, van, truck, bus, tractor trailer if that motorist can't find their vehicle and they see a tow operator or supervisor they can stop them and ask them if their vehicle was towed by the Police Department or where that vehicle is or may be. That person is now supposed to check there tablet to see if it is on their screen as it should be.

All tow operators within traffic have a tablet in their tow truck and when you pull out or before you're supposed to put in your information about the vehicle you're impounding so if a motorist should stop you to question you can answer them. All your information must be logged in the tablet although it's more of a computer. If you stop a Police Officer in a car which is called a R.M.P. which means Radio Motor Patrol they also have tablets they can check to see where your vehicle is if you know your information, such as plate number, etc. rental cars, leased cars, etc. as well.

Then there is the motorist who sees his vehicle being impounded in time or the tow operator is about to pull away with his or her vehicle they can now request a V.R.A. which is a Vehicle Release Agreement which can be issued as long as a voucher number has not been generated, but if the information has been put into that tablet already the tablet does give the tow operator that voucher number and the V.R.A. will not be issued which contradicts the law made.

The V.R. A. is a summons that was made up for the motorist who catches the tow operator before leaving the curb and can get his or her vehicle released on the spot as long as the motorist has their driver's license, registration and insurance car on their person or if a rental car or leased car the agreement must be with that person, that person must be the renter or leaser or have their name(s) on the agreement or the vehicle is not supposed to be released as agreement made because many people rent and lease cars with just their names on the agreement and if anything should happen to that vehicle that person is to be responsible for that vehicle.

Rental and Leasing Company's want this as an agreement so the vehicle is not released and the rental or lease company will pick up their vehicle and the renter or leaser will have a very hard time renting or leasing in the future.

The V.R.A. will not be issued to a motorist with an International license with a rental agreement even if you can read what the agreement says. Reason being is because unless the International license is from the United States the City of New York cannot collect the revenue from other country's or suspend your license as a V.R.A. is like a moving violation, if not paid or answered within 30 days your license will be suspended, no questions asked, so if you have an International license and your vehicle is being towed, impounded, it will be towed and you will be paying the $185 to get your vehicle out of impound and calling the police will not help as the police can't help or do anything to help you other than maybe drive you to the drive if that but the tow operator or supervisor are not permitted to have any unauthorized person's in the department vehicle whereas the police are since they do make arrest.

The issue with the motorist before the V.R.A's were then called jumpers, the vehicles were not permitted to be dropped, they must be towed regardless, then it became a law that if the motorist showed up in time they can get a V.R.A. many times it wasn't the motorist who stopped the driver and if the police were passing them by or stopped that person will be arrested for obstruction of government administration.

Years ago I had a motorist not permitted to receive a V.R.A. and a passerby stopped and told the driver to get into his vehicle, because it can't be towed if he is sitting in the vehicle, he called me every curse word you can think of, I suggested he get into the car with the motorist and he kept cursing me so he did get into the motorist car with the motorist.

The outcome was when the cops got there and I spoke to the cops both of them were arrested, the passerby tried to stop himself from being arrested and then the cops questioned me and I said arrest him also for getting into the motorist vehicle waiting for the Police Department to show up and for cursing at me because he did sit in the car with the motorist, let him see how it feels now.

Also when it comes to a V.R.A. with a heavy duty tow you must be classified to be driving that vehicle meaning if that vehicle weighs over 26001 lbs. it means you need a Commercial Driver's License class B anything over 26001 lbs. means you're driving out of class which is a moving violation as well can be an arrest. Today most or all trucks have a weight of 26000 pounds avoiding the class B license.

As for motorcycles many riders don't have the "M" endorsement which means they took the road test for motorcycle and many motorcycles do get towed either because the owner takes off the license plate thinking the bike can't be towed and claims the plate gets stolen although with no plates the motorcycle is considered abandoned, no "M" endorsement means no V.R.A. even if that owner has a driver's license because they never took a road test, even if they have a learners permit.

Many so called drivers do have a learners permit, same as driving a car, it's not a driver's license, meaning the motorcycle can and will be towed unless the owner has a friend with them there at the location with them present not 15 minutes away and is willing to accept the $100 fine on their driver's license for the owner.

Another issue is when those people or motorist are scofflaws, which means you have unpaid parking summonses that are in judgment, meaning not paid, unless you have a paid receipt from the finance dept. or a contract showing you're paying off the summonses with you there in the windshield of that vehicle, and now at home. Then when that happens and your vehicle is being towed a plate check can or will be done and if found that you're a scofflaw no matter what excuses you may have your vehicle is being towed unless you can prove you have an agreement with the Sherriff or Marshall and are paying those summonses off, if no contract, no vehicle or V.R.A.

All it can take is 1 summons that goes into judgment and within 30 days you're on the list and if the Sheriff picks up your vehicle you're going to be paying a lot more than if the police department tows your vehicle. The difference is the Sheriff or Marshall and take money from you to pay off your scofflaw whereas Traffic is not permitted to because that is considered a bribe which is an arrest.

Another issue with vehicles with no plates are usually new car dealers, dealers are known for parking brand new cars on the streets as well sidewalks, bus stops, hydrants, in every violation because when the memo came down that no vehicle is to be written off the vin number because if done that summons will be sent to the last owner of that vehicle, so if you sold your used car to a gas station or car dealer and he puts that car on the streets with no plates and the Police department does a sweep of car dealers or chop shops and your car gets a summons on the vin number that summons will go to the last registered owner to that vehicle unless you can show proof that you surrendered your plates to your car as well who you sold your car to so the city goes after them for the payment on that summons.

Again just another contradicting rule, don't write any parking summonses to any vehicle with no plates on the vin number, then be told to write it because any vehicle parked on the city streets within the (5) five boroughs is considered abandoned which includes motorcycles, any vehicle.

What I have noticed with Traffic Agents are there are different kind of people writing summonses, one (1) agent will write what he wants to write, whereas others will write what they can write, others in towing have other issues with towing, one(1) will tow a car only, no trucks or anything close to a pickup truck.

I have known a tow truck driver who will only tow a car with a summons already issued summons on it, whereas if a vehicle needs a summons they won't write it, then you have other types of people who will write the summons but won't tow it because it's not a fwd. vehicle, mean the car is not a front wheel drive vehicle, whereas other drivers will tow anything including a front wheel drive vehicle.

To tow a real wheel drive vehicle or an old car can be somewhat difficult because today you must pull the linkage, if you know where it is.

Another issue with Police Officers use the old summonses, they can be written with any time written on it, any plate number written on it and who's going to question them. You can write a friend of yours and if they approach you in a professional manner and they let you know it was there vehicle you wrote that Police Officer can always change the plate number without anybody else knowing about it or it can be pulled if it wasn't turned in yet.

What many people do is interfere with the tow truck operators by saying why are you towing my car or stand in the way preventing the tow operators from doing their jobs even when it means issuing a parking summons they stand in the way so the Traffic Agent can't write or scan the vehicle, or move there tow trucks, those people can be arrested and many have for O.G.A. which means Obstructing Government Administration which means preventing that city worker from doing their jobs and if arrested an arrest can be done and usually is for a desk appearance ticket which means that person must appear in court and if they don't show up a warrant for their arrest if issued.

Many people seem to feel this is a joke till the handcuffs are on. Others know the laws and don't interfere or want to get involved because many have seen this happen. Traffic Agents are not Police Officers but as I stated some can make the arrest, which many people are not educated enough to understand this.

When a Traffic Agent who directs Traffic request the motorist information such as driver's license, registration and insurance car it means they committed a moving violation and are liable for a moving violations summons which can be issued. When the motorist refuses their papers to that Traffic Agent the local precinct is called for a sector car and when the police show up you can be arrested as well your car impounded or the summon(s) can be issued for the violation as well failure to comply which is a violation for an arrest.

What I can explain about Traffic Intersections is this, all intersections must be covered, at least the priority post because the Federal Government pays for the Traffic Agents to be at certain locations but in the field, even if the Traffic Agent is in the wrong place, the priority intersections is the priority.

If there are enough agents are out in the field then they can replace them to help move Traffic, which is very helpful to those. Directing Traffic is a very helpful job, and just like the rest of Traffic, it's a thankless job, meaning everyone hates us, although many do love us because when we are out there in the field, in the rain, snow, whatever the weather is we are out there doing what we can.

If the weather is that bad as the Police Commissioner one time took us out of the intersections because the roads were that slippery because if the cars are that slippery driving, why would you have us out there is we get hit by and run driver, why should we be out there, this is a very serious emergency situation. We all praised the Police Commissioner for doing that.

We do understand we must be out in the field but when it's that bad that nobody can see 5 feet in front of them and they are all slipping everywhere how we can be in the field without getting hurt.

What everyone seems to believe is that all we do is issue summonses, which is a major part of the job, but not the whole function. If you compare our job to a police officer's job the difference is Peace Officer Status and handcuffs and a gun.

A Traffic agent's job is extremely dangerous as well and is done (24) twenty four hours a day, (7) seven days a week which includes all holidays, same as police officers, but paid much differently. When I started working for Traffic on August 2. 1982 I was in the Department of Transportation which is a part of Finance Department all in Department Of Transportation we were forced to merge into the Police Department in 1996 because the Mayor claimed we are a law enforcement agency but the truth is the Police Department just wanted tow truck operators and mainly the budget, nothing else, nothing more.

Rumors had it that in Department Of Transportation the department needed a major cleaning up and the Police Department was the agency to do it, which it wasn't, because since the merge a lot of illegal activity has been within the Police Department with very little to do within Traffic Enforcement. Our titles and shield were changed as well to match other city agencies.

The only positive thing to happen to us in the Police Department was a restricted parking permit for most of us, not all. The city was beginning to recognize us as revenue and we are also called when needed as emergency response although we are not or ever were an emergency response, never trained for any type of emergencies of any kind because that would mean the city of New York would have to pay us all for that service which the city refuses to do.

We are eyes and ears although never recognized for the work we perform on a daily basis. We are recognized as a part of the Police Department, not as Traffic Enforcement as it should be because even in school safety they are recognized. The difference being that when we do something positive we have never been recognized where if a police officer does something positive he is now a hero, as well recognized, not us.

A Police Office can be interviewed on Television, after he or she did something supposedly courageous whereas we are not permitted or face discipline actions all within the Police Department.

I had been to 1 Police Plaza when the department had new candidates for the job as Traffic Enforcement Agent where over 500 candidates showed for their interviews, many got the approval whereas many didn't because they did not understand the function other than to say you write summonses or didn't have a driver's license or they had a problem with their driver's license and that candidate was not honest about it. I met many men and woman who were professional people who just lost their jobs and needed jobs as well benefits to support their families.

What I have seen lately is how those get promoted, most if not all by favoritism, no test except for Traffic Supervisor-1, which is the 1 St line Supervisor, a test for Traffic Supervisor-1 must be taken, no favorites at all, after that all appointed up to Traffic Manager and above, which is supposed to be a test and those of some higher ranks are provisional.

What I have also seen is that as a Supervisor I have trained others how to do their jobs and to see how they got promoted to be my Supervisor leaving me to keep showing others how to do a job where I should be getting that promotion that I'm not getting.

The Police Department is good for promoting their own, buying new vehicles for themselves, etc. using our funds leaving us to do more work on a daily basis. The Police Department has given Traffic Enforcement a lot more responsibility since we merged more than ever before and the pay is the same as the unions are now negotiating with some agents making about the same as a supervisor which has been like that for a while.

It is supposed to eight (8) twelve (12) Traffic Agents for one (1) Supervisor, not twenty (20) or more for one (1) supervisor but in the Police Department that's how much they care. When it comes to signing your agents in the field you're expected to sign all your agents even if you have to respond to an emergency situation, no excuses because nobody wants to hear any.

Within Traffic there are many good people and supervisors and then there are those that just plain suck, nasty attitude or they know somebody who can and will hurt you and not care anything about you. There are those yes people who will never say no unless they don't want to do something and they have the backup of the higher up to back them.

What I see the most by the motorist is they don't read signs other than pay at the meter not reading what the sign really says, or claim the signs are confusing or to many signs to read or what violation is in effect or can they park there because they see others parked there.

In Midtown there are many signs on the pole that you don't know what is what and your car may get towed if somebody tells that person not to park there. When they are given the answers it's usually the answer the motorist don't want to hear and many times about a permit that the average motorist don't want to hear or know about, that causes issues because many permits do cause problem's due to over abuse.

This is where Internal Affairs Bureau comes into the picture because at one (1) time the community around One Police Plaza was complaining how can a vehicle be parked illegally and get summonsed and towed and when the department tow truck tows their cars a department vehicle will park there in the same spot in violation and put the department restricted parking permit on their dash board and leave that vehicle there and nothing happens.

Now I.A.B. has department tow trucks assigned to a Sargent and they follow that Sargent around and summons writers to various boroughs and find these vehicles parked illegally and tow them to the tow pound in that borough and the motorist in most cases will pay for the tow and summons unless on official business which must be proved. No vehicles get out free without a written reason.

When it comes to the tow pounds the police department seems to believe we are A.A.A. because we must respond to dead batteries, (flat tires), we don't change flat tires, we take that department vehicle to the repair shop, no starts, lock outs, etc. When the president comes to town and all high ranking cops are in the area of where the president is going to be they all park there department vehicles wherever they want and the tow truck drivers must relocate them because they are not permitted to park the department vehicles where they leave them leaving it to the tow operators to find spots.

When it comes to movie shoots the movie companies are paying for tow truck drivers and supervisors overtime which has changed but the movie company's don't know now the supervisors and tow truck operators are now doing those details on regular time charging the movie companies for their overtime cheating the movie companies. Each movie shoot should have a Supervisor, it was doing three (3)movie shoots and then get another Supervisor, that all depends now on the overtime being given out, the Managers claim that don't have the money to have Supervisor because they may reach their time cap for overtime limits for there month.

The Manhattan Tow Pound should have unlimited overtime because there is never enough tow truck drivers or supervisors to go all around especially when there all time limits are just about over within two (2) weeks in time, that's how overtime you can make there, but then there is one (1) Traffic Manager who will argue that you make more money than he or she does make. The two pounds are doing details almost every night in all boroughs.

When it comes to the Chief of Transportations we have had a few that were questionable. We had a Chief that was Traffic happy which means he loved Traffic Agents and went out of his way to make sure things did happen in favor of Traffic whereas his predecessor was another story after he was forced to retired. That Chief was not Traffic happy and didn't care about Traffic Agents at all. He did retaliate against Traffic because his wife's car was towed being parked illegally and that Chief went out of his way to do whatever he can to hurt traffic, meaning a level-2 Traffic Agent was no longer permitted to carry or write moving violations, as the Director of Traffic's gun was taken away although nobody understood why he needed a gun because he was not a cop.

Another issue with the former Chief of Transportation was if or when a tow truck operator was involved in an accident, minor or not, in most cases the tow truck operator was found to be at fault as per the Chief of Transportation regardless if the driver wasn't at fault and that driver had to do intersection duties for 30 days, also be given a Command Discipline regardless and then attend a class at Floyd Bennett Field then if he or she passes they can now a department vehicle again because you must be certified to drive any Police Department vehicle and the only place to be certified was at Floyd Bennett Field, even if a bicycle or motorcycle, scooter, etc. Regardless, you must be certified. Another part of Traffic Division was called T.I.U. which stood for Traffic Intelligence Unit which had Traffic Agents level-4 patrol the highways and bridges, one(1) agent was working and he observed a vehicle being driven recklessly as he decided to do a car stop.

The Agent found the motorist to be D.W.I and was issued summonses and the motorist began yelling at the agent saying do you know who I am or who my uncle is to where the agent said it really didn't matter who your uncle is as she was given summonses which before that agents tour was over T.I.U. was dissolved because that female yelling was the niece of the former Chief of the Department who had all summonses dismissed and made sure Traffic Agents no longer carry as well issue moving violations.

So if your drunk and driving and have a relative who is a high ranking cop and you commit a serious violation it will most likely be dismissed before the media can get their hands on it, but if was off duty Traffic Agent or Supervisor or Manager was stopped everything goes from arrest, to handcuffs, to assaults, etc. even though your called a M.O.S. which stands for Member Of Service.

Another issue was a few years back a Chief who worked out of 30 St was having an affair with a Sargent although the Chief was married the affair kept going and it was on the overnight tour as I understand, the Sargent and Chief were very close since the Sargent was the Chief's driver, driving the Chief wherever he needed to go and then some to where the Sargent found out she was pregnant by the Chief, the Chief now applied for a new job down South and when it was time to go to the new job he quietly retired leaving the Sargent not just pregnant but not knowing the Chief was retiring. The Chief lost the job down South and tried to get his old job back and the Police Department denied his request so no job and a pregnant Sargent and still married.

This type of stuff happens everywhere but in the Police Department, a department that was supposed to clean up us D.O.T. works now supposed M.O.S. nothing has changed, it only got a whole lot worse.

Now Traffic Intelligence Unit, is now called T. S. O., which stands for Traffic Special Operations which responds to emergency situations in all 5 boroughs, directing traffic as needed.

Another recent issue is a Traffic Agent who is very close to the Deputy Director was promoted to a TS- 1 St line supervisor, now being a TS-1 and was having problems with the vacation request although approved and his tour which was ordered to make it the A.M. tour was denied his vacation before the Traffic Manager felt that agent didn't deserve to have it at the time requested because now that agent was promoted and because P.D.'s rules contradict saying vacation goes by seniority in rank although approved prior to the promotion which must stand the Traffic Manager felt that as the manager that there word over rules what the Deputy Director is ordering done. The issue is the driver is also Spanish and so are the Deputy Director's so it's obvious which way this situation goes.

That agent, now supervisor was transferred out due to that Traffic Manager harassing that agent and the nonsense which is known everywhere that this Manager is transferred to.

Since 2014 many M.O.S. within Traffic or the Police Department have been forced to retire due to nonsense being sent down the chain of command because higher ranks felt they needed to leave and let new people take their jobs over, not enough summonses being written or tows being called in or towed in, assignments had been changed.

Rules within the Police Department change every day just like the weather and if you don't know the rules you're in trouble. Rules and new codes cards are made up basically yearly as well.

Another issue with the Police Department is domestic abuse, the department does not tolerate it or drugs or alcohol, but when it comes to alcohol you will sent to the farm to be cleaned up for 30 days, no phones or any outside communications at all.

Today within Police Department many police officers work off duty employment working for U.P.S., Fed- Ex as well other company's by sitting in the trucks so they don't get summonsed or towed. Reason being is because of what is in the trucks of value so an off duty police officer is sitting in the truck although not permitted by the Police Department because any M.O.S. within the Police Department is required to fill out a form called Off Duty Employment so the department knows what you're doing and for whom, within Traffic it can be a Command Discipline or suspension but as a police officer those rules change, some due to rank because there are many high ranking cops who do moon light as well.

Many of these companies have agreements with the city where they pay $5.00 for ever summons they receive regardless how much the summons is, even if the summons is $115.00, they only pay $5.00, but if the vehicle gets towed, they must pay the whole tow fee, either $185.00 for a regular tow or a $370 for the heavy duty tow. If you have that agreement with the city you can't fight the summons or you lose your agreement with the city which is part of the deal.

If you do get a parking summons and towed and must go to the tow pound to redeem your vehicle many motorist will make a claim stating their vehicle was damaged even before getting to the vehicle thinking that they can make a claim against the city for prior damage not caused by the tow truck.

I have seen and heard motorist needing a pass to get there documentation from their vehicle only to say they want to make a damage claim without even seeing the vehicle thinking they will get money back from the city for damages that were there as well make a theft claim. A theft claim is a very serious allegation to make because now I.A.B. must be called and get involved and now making a false police report can lead to an arrest.

Many people do claim they had a lot of money in their vehicle and then when its proven the vehicle was not entered being the vehicle is a front wheel drive vehicle and the parking brakes were never on, it now become proof the motorist is a liar trying to make a false claim against the city as it has been proven many times. But then there is never an arrest to the motorist theft claim, never. A legit damage claim can be but don't have to be is a broken oil pan, or transmission pan, door locks, etc.

All towed vehicle must have a voucher and on that voucher it will show a diagram of a vehicle which the tow operator must show all damages as well on the field inspection book which is a green multi page book which must be filled out prior to towing showing all damages and property visible.

If you left property in your glove compartment and your doors are locked and the car is front wheel drive then now I.A.B. will or may give you a 2nd chance to admit guilt and allow you to check at your home to see if you left your valuables there because if you insist in claiming a claim and your vehicle is dusted for finger prints which can or will come up negative, your chances now of arrest are very positive to happen.

It has happened that any car is towed and the tow operator can't lock that particular vehicle so now that Supervisor must have it relocated to the Manhattan Tow Pound or to the borough that vehicle belongs in to be secured or face consequences.

During my years in the tow pounds I have seen and heard many stories that anybody can tell were made up and warning the motorist of what or will happen has no phase on them till it happens. Just like being caught with a bogus parking permit or being towed with it in your vehicle because when that happens if you can't show proof as a city worker or the permit is yours, your under arrest for possession of a forged instrument, because everybody claims there brother in law or some guy gave it to them which can mean jail time and many do give up that person not to face time. Many are legit and then many aren't and when they aren't legit expect the worse.

I had a brand new Fiat towed with an old expired Police Department parking permit in the window and her boyfriend was a Captain within the Department and when he I.D.'d himself to I.A.B. he got his permit back and everything was just about squashed, he paid the tow fee and summons and his girlfriend tried to make a complaint, then she tried to make an issue, which back fired on her.

I have had many issues within my (31) thirty one years working with some of the best people and the worse and I can say even if you hate your coworker as many do when it comes to support many will come to your support as they would expect the same of you. For the year of 2014 the Police Department has been forcing all rank Police Officers and Traffic Enforcement Agents and Supervisors out claiming they have been employees long enough and it's time for new blood to take over although only rumored and is happening.

Another part of Traffic now is P.C.U. which was a part of D.O.T. which was Parking Control Unit who only wrote parking meters and parking permits, which also meant P.D. parking permits. P.C.U. wrote everybody and Traffic agents took the heat for it. P.C.U. also got paid much more money than Traffic agents which also included higher ranks and them also merged into the Police Department with the understanding that when they merged in the P.D. they can never be promoted, which is a union issue which has never been disputed yet.

Summonses that are no longer permitted to be written are 12 inches from the curb for what reason makes no sense. Trucks parked in a No Standing zone or in a No Standing 4 P.M. x 7 P.M. Mon thru Fri with a truck over 12 inches from the curb can't be issued a summons for obstructing traffic because we are no longer allowed to issue them as well for blocking driveway except with your immediate Supervisor.

Same for spillback summonses which are really a moving violation, the city made a parking summons for spillback a few years back in 2008 because a moving violation the State collects all the revenue on that summons whereas if a parking summons is issued the city gets it all. The city made a code of (09) which was verified with an Administrative Law judge for parking advising how to write such a summons that if the motorist is sitting and not moving in the intersection with the vehicle in drive with the motor running blocking the intersection, blocking oncoming traffic, from going it was now a parking summons and now Traffic Agents were ordered to go into traffic and write those summonses with a Supervisor standing nearby and sometimes a police officer who was supposed to be directing traffic standing on the sidewalk allowing this to happen with no say in the matter. But from what I have heard that is now over, no more writing those summons, or maybe they do when it's necessary. If the motorist made any attempts on assaulting that Traffic agent that police officer was there to make that arrest if he wanted to or not.

When it comes to Commercial vehicles there are many rules about them often can be contradicting. Observation times, the city says (30) thirty minutes is enough time for loading and unloading, then it can be one (1) hours depending on that particular area, then it became commercial metered zones which most people don't read signs because one sign says pay the meter not knowing the parking spaces are strictly for commercial parking only.

Commercial vehicles are never observed correctly, Traffic Agents are using time, not using chalk on the tires to show if that particular vehicle was been moved which makes it easier to tow.

When it comes to commercial vehicles the rules are, posted permanent signs on both sides of the doors showing the name of the company with the address three (3) inches long not the same color as the car in contrast, no back seat or seat fittings, which includes station wagons with folded seats, putting a blanket in the back always helped. There are different types of commercial vehicles, Commercial, IRP, ARP, APP, TRUCK, etc. The times Commercial vehicles can be parked are thirty (30) minutes unless you're on a parking meter that says Commercial Parking only, then you may be parked there.

The code cards are always changing and a new code for tractor trailers for parking at night after 9 P.M. x 5 A.M. is parking in a residential area was never permitted at all and was a $65 summonses and now there are 2 codes which does have a difference because 1 is for tractor trailers whereas the other is for trucks and the 1 for tractor trailers it's a new code with a $265 summonses with a 2 ND time around going for $500, which are both a towable violation. Another violation for commercial vehicles is 3 hour storage which can be anytime within 24 hours 7 days. A commercial vehicle may not be parked in the city streets past 9 P.M. except for emergency heating and air conditioning vehicles which is posted in the traffic rules, if read.

I was doing these details a lot with the various precincts in all 5 boroughs of the city on overtime as 311 complaints as well community board complaints which went to their local precincts, all vehicles would be issued parking summonses and if the motorist would be around, spoken to, asking them not to park the trucks or tractor trailers on the residential streets because the residents were complaining because late at night they could not find parking or the diesel fumes were effecting their health or the refrigerator trailers would start up automatically waking them up in the middle of the night, which went ignored in many cases.

That's where I came into the picture with my crew of heavy duty tow operators which included men as well woman who knew what to do and did it regardless. I had my regular men I would use and I would always ask others who always had excuses as to why they could not do the details so I asked my regular men and sometimes I would take others who wanted to do them to get the experience with my regular men who had the experience and expertise and I would set up a date to meet at the precinct, set up the strategy, if we never worked with that precinct before, go to the location of most complaints, make sure the summonses were correct, and hook up vehicles, and tow them to the tow pound in the most cases in the borough if they had room or a tow pound with the most room for at least 6 or 10 tractor trailers, if not then we went to another tow pound within the 5 boroughs, which was usually Brooklyn.

All Commanding Officers were extremely happy with our results addressing their complaints and in many cases there community board members were there observing us addressing their complaints watching us towing the trucks, buses, tractor trailers they were complaining about and thanking us for our work, which is very rare. These details were an eight (8) hour details and all overtime and during the detail we would take a (30) thirty minute break to eat something quick.

The Sargent or above would ask us if there was anything they can do for us in return and we would ask for a letter of recognition which they agreed to but we never received in writing, as requested. I gave my men that letter of recognition in writing although I never got it myself as I was later forced to retire and now those men I had were very experienced at what we did don't want to do those details anymore seeing how it got and how the Police Department is.

A vehicle with multiple summonses, what does that mean? Does it mean having (3) three summonses on it at one time, although you can get three(3) summonses at one(1) time for expired meter, expired registration or inspection sticker or missing plate but not according to the police department, it means if you park your car at the exact location every day or almost every day and get summons every day or almost there is a report that is done within traffic that the 1 St line supervisor gets that shows that, not even the 2 ND line supervisor will get this report but will know about it, what will happen is your plate number appears showing your plate number at the same location usually a meter, same meter number and is in violation the supervisor will call the tow pound in that borough for a department tow truck to impound your vehicle because it becomes an integrity issue.

I responded to this type of issue and the motorist did show up in time and I explained the situation to him and he agreed not to park there anymore whereas the next motorist yelled and screamed and could not be calmed down.

In this case a V.R.A. can be issued as long as the motorist has the driver's license, registration, insurance with them, no excuses, and no plate checks done. This is the same as a moving violation but no extra summonses issued if the papers are not provided, meaning no registration or insurance, no V.R.A. V.R.A. is a Vehicle Release Agreement which the tow operator, motorist, supervisor must sign, to dismiss this summons you must get the parking summons dismissed 1 St, then have the V.R.A. summons dismissed.

If the motorist wants to call the police it won't make any difference because they can' change anything except arrest the motorist for O.G.A. which again is obstructing government administration. If the parking summons is lowered in amount where your still paying your still liable for that V.R.A. unless that administrative law judge is willing to lower that fine as well, which should be done in person. This is a way for the city to make revenue at the tax payer's expense with a poor excuse.

Another violation is parking a vehicle for over 7 days straight without moving it which can be a handicap vehicle, which I have seen and had to tow which does not have to be handicap, there was no street cleaning in that area and around that vehicle was loaded with dirt and garbage as it would be with a detached trailer or tractor trailer that has been sitting for days or weeks, it's illegal, especially a detached trailer, which is also a fire hazard. Traffic, which nobody does anything about if you have a Commercial Driver's License (C.D.L.) then you know what I'm talking about to move it to release the brakes you need air pressure. No tractor attached it can cause a fire or it can be just a fire hazard, some drivers do just disconnect the tractor, but it does stay appearing to be hooked up to a detached trailer.

Vehicle registrations, there was a 49 that came down a few years back saying if the vehicles registration expired (1) one month you can tow that vehicle, then it became a secondary summons, meaning you needed a main violation like no parking or no standing, no stopping, or fire hydrant, etc. I had vehicles towed for expired registrations if expired over (2) two months after I ran the plate only to find out there was nothing on file meaning the registration was no longer legal, expire inspection stickers were similar meaning expired 30 days you can tow by a 49 then it became a secondary summons, meaning you needed a main violation which got confusing as to why this all started as a violation to be towed as a safety issue, then it became a secondary violation although I had vehicles towed if they were expired for over (3) three months expired due to a safety reasons and to redeem their vehicle the owner must have their vehicle towed out due to safety reasons.

Mismatch plates is another issue the plates don't match the registration is reason to tow the vehicle because the plates don't belong to that vehicle. Traffic agents can no longer issue summonses for blocking a driveway even if you can prove it's your driveway whereas a police officer can and traffic was permitted to tow that vehicle, no more. Now if a vehicle is blocking your driveway only a police officer can issue that summons for blocking your driveway and then you must call a tow company to tow that vehicle, the police department cannot give out any tow company's information as a integrity, feeling that police officer or Traffic agent will get something in return or gratuity for giving out phone number for the business in return.

Many people want to know how to beat a parking summons or even a moving violation. Read posted signs and stop saying the sign is so far away, more than 30 feet away because that sounds ridiculous. Beating a parking summons can be easy if the summons is altered or has multiple boxes marked, meaning if the state says N.Y. or N.J. and both are "X" out and 1 is circled, or was just written wrong that summons is no good because its altered, that summons is a legal document and must be a true, legal summons.

Many people don't try to beat these summonses claiming they just don't have the time they need. Anybody can send the Parking Violations bureau there summons to beat it if they do it right, make copies of their original summons and keep their copies, don't send Parking Violations bureau copies, unless it's there registration, send them originals and you should be the winner of that summons.

If the summons is marked pas (meaning passenger) plate and it's a comm, (meaning commercial) then the summons should be dismissed, with the copy of the registration included showing so. No summons should show C/O meaning (corner of) because there are eight (8) corners if not, for (4) as many think, so which corner is it of? How long can you leave your commercial vehicle parked at the same location? The rules say thirty minutes (30) other say one (1) hour or actually three (3) hours, it all depends.

It's either an exact address or exact footage, meaning W/S Coney Island Ave 20 Ft S/O Ave K, which is exact footage for a Bus Stop, otherwise that summons is no good and should be dismissed no matter who wrote it.

Our previous mayor changed our city around by making Times Square more of a tourist attraction by having the streets closed so tourist can sit and drink coffee or take pictures whereas others can take a bike ride with a City bike that the mayor gave his son in law the contract to which makes no sense to because these city bikes are in bad locations that if vehicles can't be parked there why can bicycles be there? They are all over the city which do cause motor vehicle accidents and injure pedestrians and can damage to the bicycles. Ex: A no standing zone is where nobody is permitted to park a vehicle even if a passenger or the motorist is sitting in the vehicle, so why would anybody put a rack of bicycles there? Many are in dangerous places and they are only to generate revenue not caring about anybody personal being.

I was checking my code card the Police Department issued to me which shows there are 81 parking violations which many are never used and one (1) that is made up when a violations is not posted, that code is # 99 which is used for parking a vehicle for over seven (7) consecutive days straight without moving and can be used as needed. If the violation is not posted on a summons there is an open box to print the violation in with the price, code, violation, etc.

There are (3) three high priced violations that people always ignore and when caught complain about how short a time they were parked there not caring about the motorist who really need those spaces. The highest is for a tractor trailer parked overnight in a residential area, code is # 06 at $265 the 1 set time, $500 the 2 ND time, then comes No Parking Handicap Zone which is $180, code #27 and then pedestrian ramp which is code # 67 at $165.

A pedestrian ramp is not on every corner as many think but when a street like Shore Blvd in Manhattan Beach or Ave U from Hendrickson St to East.38 Street that has 1 side of the street that goes for blocks whereas if you cross the street the blocks to have an intersection the side with the long block will have a pedestrian ramp made for wheel chairs to be able to have the access to cross over.

Movie shoots are done all the time located in all (5) five boroughs. Movie shoots are done with the department tow trucks to remove the cars that are parking legally, they are moved to other spots so they can park their own vehicles where it need be and can be issued a damage claim if the motorist feels his or her car was damaged by a department tow truck, but the department tow truck must be accountable in writing he or she did that damage. A scratch can be given a damage claim unless there is proof that department tow truck did that damage. Either way a damage claim will be issued regardless but now the damage claim book will state NTR, means (not tow related), so you can get the damage claim but that's about it.

All tow truck drivers have a green book which is called Vehicle Inspection Book, which all drivers must carry and filled out before they pull away with that vehicle showing all damages as well visible property showing inside that car, no showing in the glove compartment because we never go in the glove compartment, its close or locked before that vehicle ever moved from their original spots, anybody that makes a claim saying that damage was there afterwards is a no good claim no matter what that motorist claims that Field Inspection book says it all. Many cars are front wheel drive and the brakes are off so to move the car is usually easy, pick it up, and move it, many vehicles are moved across the street or around the corner, someplace there is a parking spot.

As for handicap parking permits there are 2 different kinds, one(1) is from the State which only allows the owner a permit which goes on the rear view mirror, a blue permit which is only good at off street parking spaces, like a supermarket parking space, which is off street, whereas the city Special Vehicle Identification known as a SVI permit is a permit that is about 8 1/2 x 11 which sits on the dashboard of the car and you can park almost anyplace, except in a bus stop, hydrant, no standing anytime, no stopping, double parking, etc.. Otherwise you can park on an expired meter, street cleaning, and no standing except authorized vehicles.

If you do get a summons for something you're not supposed to be parked at with the S.V.I. permit you can see the Administrative Law judge with proof of what you were doing and your handicap and no promises but the judge may give you some leniency if only late by a few minutes as long as your parked in a No Parking violation, but if it a No Standing violation the judges are usually lenient to a point.

If you park near a fire hydrant you must be fifteen (15) feet away from the hydrant either side, not eight (8) or (10) feet because as funny as it may seem your still not (15) fifteen feet and if a fire should happen the fire department will do whatever it takes to get to that hydrant which can mean going thru your windows if need be, that summons is $115 as well towable if anything is left over if a fire.

As for fighting a summons by mail is a waste of time because you will probably be found guilty in many cases if you know how to plead your case with proof which your copy of your registration, or pictures whereas in person is your best bet.

Fighting a moving violation you must appear in court, no exceptions, you can postpone your case for another day, so can the police officer, but if you don't show up your license will be suspended. When you plead your case with a moving violation many Administrative Law judges will hear you out although may will have a conversation with their secretary and claim they are listening to you but the truth is they already have you guilty no matter what your excuse is, you're guilty. You're going to be to pay and you can appeal if you wish. Administrative Law Judges are like Traffic Agents and Police officers, they must find so many guilty and then can dismiss so many within good reasons.

As for violations there are many different types of violations within and all motorist don't care about signs because they are ignored especially when the sign says No Stopping Anytime and the motorist stops even to talk on their cell phone. The reason for No Stopping is because if an emergency arises at that location which is a prime location with very important dignitaries if the fire department must get it or Police Department or F.B.I. or whatever agency they must be permitted access to that location with no obstacles in their way or can be arrested.

There are also many locations with a No Standing sign posted which also goes ignored because the motorist will give themselves permission or say I will only be (2) tow seconds. The reason a No Standing sign can be posted is because of a driveway to a parking lot, it makes it difficult seeing when a SUV is there or any vehicle is parked there and when the motorist is attempting to exit the parking lot can't see causing an accident due to the vehicle being parking in a No Standing zone. There are different types of No Standing zones besides those. I can explain them all but I believe everybody knows them or if you're not sure what they mean should read the driver's manual again as it changes.

I'm sure there are questions many motorist may have and if I'm contacted at will I will either answer your questions I will be writing another be at writing another book with the new sentence as I hope my answers here are correct and what everybody wants to hear or read as I was forced to tell the truth about what really goes on within Traffic as a 2 ND line Traffic Supervisor being forced out due to nonsense within by a higher up Manager with the over abuse of power of authority.

CPR is on all Police Department vehicles and preached to all members of the Police Department and preached to every department member to be used to everybody, coworkers, public, supervisors, etc. Cursing from a supervisor to a subordinate is not acceptable and is ignored when reported to their supervisors or even E.E.O who says it a union issue which are ignorant who don't represent their members, just collect union dues and laugh at complaints being made because they are friends with those the complaints are about which are higher up as well management.

The Police Department needs to take a good look in the mirror because we now have a new mayor who sees what he wants to see as well his new police commissioner who claims there is no quota although I beg to differ, although the word quota is not the phrase used, there is.

A union rep from a tow pound within DC-37 told me publicly, corruption is running very wild within the Police Department and having an Inspector was the last thing the Police Department wanted because within time either a lot of brass will be forced to retire or be caught doing things they should not of been doing, some have already and not publicized.

When we merged into the Police Department some high ranking cop came up with an idea that when a vehicle is impounded for being illegally parked and the motorist shows up to redeem his or her vehicle run the driver's license as it was being done already, reason being a lot of people had warrants for their arrest out as well for domestic abuse or child support being or a dead beat dad or spousal support. When the motorist showed up to redeem their vehicle the driver's license would be ran and if it came up as a hit the motorist was set up at the exit way when they produced there receipt showing they paid the tow fee, a squad car would be waiting for them to leave the tow pound, do a car stop and arrest the motorist for whatever the reasons were and the vehicle would be towed back into the tow pound all because that receipt was never stamped as allowed to be.

I do remember seeing a vehicle towed in to the Manhattan Tow Pound, paying the tow feel and getting that vehicle out, not knowing the Police Department was sitting at the south gate waiting for that particular vehicle to leave not knowing that person has multiple summons on him or her for no payment or being a dead beat dad or whatever the warrant were for, till that stopped because I do believe it was illegal to be done back then when we just merged into the Police Department.

That stopped after many motorist had lawyers who found the Police Department was doing was entrapment, suing the City and Police Department, which eventually stopped.

As for DC-37 a union rep also sued the commanding officer of parking enforcement district after he was involved in a minor accident which he was not found at fault but after having an accident prevention meeting at 34 St with all commands that representative was found to half ½ at fault meaning he was now told he must direct traffic for 30 days, not 45. That lead to issues being a union representative as other union reps and non-union reps had accidents which they had to be in an intersection for 45 days going down eventually to 30, then 20 days after the union rep sued the commanding officer for harassment by the commanding officer having a I.C.O. from all commands go to that agents intersection to sign him every day which now includes supervisors, this all happen because of the Chief Of Transportation, he had issues with Traffic, and this is how bad he hated us all.

All Traffic agents on intersection patrol carry a paper field patrol and this union rep had to carry at least three (3) field patrols because each time he was signed by his supervisor or Integrity Control Officer (I.C.O.) as an agent you're required to update your field patrol putting yourself back on intersection patrol or issuance if issuing summonses. The commanding officer lost his cases in court because he had more than one(1) case, more like two(2)or even three(3), all lost, and won by DC-37 union rep.

Union Presidents are also in legal trouble due to missing funds or loans given out that were not supposed to of been done, which is a Federal Offense. Funds must be accountable with the Union Hall books available to be checked at any time and if refused it can cause legal problems.

Being a liar as well two (2) faced is a requirement within the Police Department as well a lot of cursing, go into any police precinct within the five(5) boroughs and you will hear Officers, Sergeants, even Lieutenants, as well Captains, etc., cursing worse than sailors publically not caring who hears them in front of woman, female officers, female Sargent's, female Lieutenants, female Captains and even higher whereas if Traffic should do that practice a command discipline will be instituted immediately, if not sooner.

High rank Traffic Managers do curse at subordinates publically as it happened to me publically as well other supervisors and my union did nothing but laugh although supposedly reported it to the Deputy Director of Traffic to direct the complaint to the higher rank Traffic Manager who was transferred, so nothing happened.

What Traffic agents and all supervisors do acknowledge is we thank the motorist because without them we would not have a job, it may be a thankless job but it pays the bills. If you look around New York City has the highest traffic congestion or one of the highest and not being able to control the traffic would mean longer times for emergency vehicles to have to respond to any type of emergency.

Longer times to get home from work or longer to get away for a holiday weekend or even a vacation much needed, whereas if there were no Traffic Agents those people who block up those heavy congested intersections would sit there forever if not longer. Sometimes a Traffic Agent does have problems directing the traffic because the motorist just refuses to listen to them which causing problems which could have been avoided.

Many motorist want to pick a fight with a Traffic Agent thinking nothing will happen till the motorist finds out they are under arrest or just want to pick an argument for something that is not the agents fault, such as a parking summons issued by somebody else even by Sanitation for street cleaning whereas if the police officer did the exact same thing the Traffic Agent did, there would be no argument because the motorist knows they can be arrested, some care whereas many don't.

As I stated many of all Traffic Agents look like police officers by the uniforms they wear and can be misidentified as such. Now I have heard the agents will be getting new uniforms, wearing a neon colored green so the city showed there colors even more. What's next? Today many motorists can't tell the difference.

Now for traffic accidents, all Traffic Agents are now doing all accident reports due to the new Chief of Transportation. They are now permitted to do the reports, since it all started back around Jan. 2015 of this year, trained to them, which now makes it better for all of us and faster than waiting for cops to show up, not saying Police are slow but when a Traffic Agents does the report it makes up for time that can't always be there when you really need it the most.

Now for trying to beat a parking ticket, it can be somewhat easy, maybe. 1 thing is read the summons carefully because many motorist take off their summons and put it on your car making it appear you got a ticket, then it's their ticket. Read the summons to check it, plate # must be your summons, then check the rest of your summons carefully, check the date registration expires, body type, color, location, everything on that summons is now yours unless you can prove it's not.

If you received a summons be sure it is yours, not like to lent the vehicle to your friend and he don't know anything about it, because by the time you get that summons it's probably yours and he is denying it.

Sign can be read but you must be very careful, what and how, you're reading that sign, it can by one (1) long block which can have just one (1) sign to cover it, that whole block. Many people see nothing and then try to claim it like the way they tell Traffic agents that sign is around twenty feet (20) away, it's too far to read. If twenty (20) feet is too far, you need to get something else other than a car to drive. Then they curse out that Traffic Agent or Police Officer for their own mistakes. If the sign contradicts, then you can win your case as long as you can prove your case, meaning take pictures showing it contradicts. Not saying there are too many sign on that traffic pole, like in Manhattan a traffic pole can have as many as six (6) or seven (7) signs on that one (1) pole saying everything, which is very confusing to the average person who is trying to read it.

Signs are everywhere, if you can read them especially in Manhattan, good luck, at least it depends on where in Manhattan you are, or live. The thing is to try to do is find legal parking spot, like a parking lot or garage, it's the cheapest place to park as long as there are lights in this place, or area and you don't want to be mugged or get hurt. Hydrants again must be fifteen (15) feet away in both directions no double parking near that fire hydrant. Trucks are great for double parking or obstructing traffic in No Standing Mon Thru Fri 4 P.M. x 7 P.M. or No Stopping Mon Thru Fri 4 P.M. If no signs on that particular block and I do say what I'm explaining then you can park at that spot.

There are always those signs that don't have any hours, meaning if that sign says No Standing, with no hours posted, the sign says (No Standing) period, it don't have to be No Standing, it can mean any sign, so check pout the signs before you park there, this is especially in Manhattan. Tourist be aware because they are biggest ones to lose especially with an International License with a V.R.A. because their vehicle or rental car is on the hook because they must pay, no V.R.A.'s are available to them.

Parking your car in Manhattan before 6 P.M. if you're in Midtown Manhattan, those sign can be confusing because the sign that reads pay the meter are for the commercial vehicle to park there if you read the sign there you would have read it correctly. As the former mayor once said Manhattan is like a pot of gold, you just have to read the sign carefully or your screwed.

You can always park where you are as long as there are just one sign saying its safe which you can read the sign carefully. If there is more than one sign on that pole read it carefully because you may not be reading it the way it should be read. Don't just read the sign that says park here because it may mean don't, because many sign are confusing to others who are not familiar with that area. Many people do park at the signs that do say one (1) hours parking, then after that the signs say No Standing from 4 P.M X 7 P.M. so as much money you can put in that meter the sign still reads No Standing, so in other words don't park there because it's your job to carefully read the signs and don't be towed.

What I do say is that many people do see the sign that says" PAY HERE" the thing with that is be sure it's really for cars and not for Commercial Vehicles because in Midtown that's what the signs do say and when you park there you can be towed unless you have a S.V.I. parking permit, except on West. 38 Street – West. 41 Streets between 6 Avenue thru 8 Avenues, no handicap parking permits permitted there just be sure you're not at a No Standing, No Stopping, Hydrant, or Bus Stop, Crosswalk, etc. if you are, prepared for the worse, a summons. The reason the worse is because many of us do have to work for a living and if anybody does get a summons and they are really handicap, can't walk, or whatever there handicap is then they will be trouble because the news loves this type of story's showing how Traffic Enforcement towed this persons car with a handicap parking permit displayed in his or her windshields.

If you do get towed check out your tow pound will be opened because if you don't read the signs and I did post it all for everybody to read, then it's all your fault. This is something I'm trying to avoid for you.

Here are the location to which if your vehicle does get towed, now you can call or just show up if you know your vehicle is really there.

Manhattan Tow Pound

Pier 76
West 38 Street / 12 Ave
212-971-0770-or 72
The pound is open 24 hrs. And it closes on Sundays at 5 A.M.

Brooklyn Navy Yard; entrance is at the corner of Sand / Navy Street

Brooklyn Tow Pound
Sand Street / Navy Street
718-237-3300
Hours of operations
Monday –Friday 8 A.M. – 10 P.M. Sundays- **CLOSED**

Upper Manhattan

If your car was towed to 203 Pound you must go to Pier 76 located at W. 38 St / 12 Ave, pay for your car there, and take the receipt back to 203 St to get your car back.

All before 7 P.M. because this pound closes at 8 P.M.
203 St / 9 Ave
Open from 7 A.M. – 8 A.M. 12P.M.
212—569-9099
Saturdays & Sundays - **CLOSED**

Queens Tow Pound

31-22 College Point Boulevard, Flushing N.Y. 11354

718-359-6200

Hours of Operations

Monday thru Friday 8 A.M. – 10 P.M.

Sunday – **CLOSED**

Bronx Tow Pound

745 East. 141 Street between Bruckner Expressway & East River

718-585-1391

Hours of Operation

Monday – Friday 8 A.M. – 10 P.M.

Saturday 8 A.M. – 3 P.M.

Sunday – **CLOSED**

On the following days the NYCPD tow pounds are **CLOSED** and people will NOT be able to redeem vehicles.

+ New Year's Day
+ Memorial Day
+ 4 Th of July
+ Labor Day
+ Thanksgiving Day
+ Christmas Day

I am writing in the codes and I am explaining them to you to see in case anybody gets a summons. I am sending out the codes so you can see them and possibly win your case(s). All codes have a (408) as a sub section.

14) No Standing (C) which means no standing. Nobody can be parked in a no standing or even sitting in a car when it in effect.

16) No Standing Except trucks (K) (2) means No standing except trucks (except for handicap vehicles) nobody can be parked at No Standing except trucks. Or legal permits.

17) No Standing except Authorized Vehicles (c) (4) nobody can be parked at this location except for those who are authorized.

19) No Standing Bus Stop (C-) (3) which means nobody can be at this location at any time.

20) No parking (d) which means No Parking, those who have a handicap parking permit are permitted to park and the permit MUST be visible as well other parking permits, which MUST be authorized to be parked there.

21) No Parking (D) (1) Street cleaning means No Parking for street cleaning. Only those who have handicap parking permits are permitted to park there.

27) No Parking except handicap plates or permits (d) (3), means that nobody should be parked there, respect the handicap parking.

31) No Standing Commercial Metered Zone (I) (3) (ii) Means nobody can be parked here except for a commercial vehicles with money in the meter.

34) Expired Meter (h) (2)

37) Expired Muni Meter (H) (10)

38) Failure to Display Muni Meter Receipt (H) (10)

40) Fire Hydrant (E) (2) (indicate Feet) must be 15 feet away or less to receive a summons.

46) Double Parked (F) (1)

67) Pedestrian Ramp (F) (7) nobody can be parked in a pedestrian ramp, due to handicaps.

70) Reg. Stkr Missing/Exp (J) (3) (NYS Only)

71) Insp. Stkr Missing/ Expired (J) (6) (NYS Only

74) Missing Plates (J) (2) NYS Only OR Improperly Display Plates (Any State) (Specify)

78) Nighttime Pkg Comm. Vehicle Residential St (K) (6) (9 P.M. – 5 A.M.)

06) Nighttime Pkg Tractor –Trailer, Comb (K) (6), Tractor Trailer detached or Semi-Trailer or Semi-trailer 1 time is ($250) 2 ND time $500.

SIGN RELATED VIOLATIONS

10) No Stopping (B)

11) No Standing (C) (5) (except Hotel Loading)

12) No Standing (C) (1) Snow Emergency

13) No Standing (C) (2) Taxi Stand

18) No Standing Bus Lane (F) (4)

89) No Standing (I) (4) Exc. Trucks/Vans with Comm. Plates (Garment Dist... Non Truck)

22) No Pkg (D) (6) Ex Hotel Loading)

23) No Pkg (D) (2) Taxi Stand

24) No Pkg (D) (5) Ex Authorized vehicles

25) No STD C (6) Community Van Stop

26) No STD C (7) For- Hire Vehicle Stop

28)@Overtime Standing Diplomat & Consul Vehicle(C) (8) (ii) 30 min. limit D Decals Only

39) @Overtime Pkg- (D) Limited Time Posted

64) No Standing (C) (8) (I) (A) Ex.Consul/ Diplomat Plates D/S Decals Only

65) @Overtime Standing(C) (8) (I) (B) Diplomat & Consul Veh. 30 min Limit D Decals Only

68) No Parking (A) (1) in compliance with posted sign

81) No Standing(C) (8) (ii) ex Consul – C, Diplomat A & D Decal 30 min limit

METER VIOLATIONS

04) Bus Meter Zone (I) (6)

32) @ Overtime Pkg (H) (3) at Missing /Broken Meter

33) #@Feeding Meter (H) (5) Get meter # & time 1 St Obs.

35) Selling/Offering Merchandise for sale (H) (8) (Metered Parking Space)

45) Traffic Lane (E) (1) this summons is no longer issued by Traffic Enf.

48) Bike Lane (E) (9)

50) Crosswalk (E) (5)

51) Crosswalk (E) (5)

52) Intersection (E) (4)

53) Safety Zone (F) (6)

55) Tunnel/Elevated Roadway (E) (7)

56) Divided Highway (E) (8)

57) Blue Zone (I) (1)

58) Marginal Street/ Water Front (G) (3)

60) Angle Street (M) (2)

61) Wrong Way (M) (1)

62) Beyond Marked Spot (D) (4)

63) Nighttime STD or Pkg in a park (F) (3)

66) Detached Trailer (K) (4)

77) Parked Bus (except in designated area) (M) (5)

80) Missing equipment (specify) (N) (8)

91) Vehicle for Sale (N) (1) Dealers Only)

92) Washing/Repairing Vehicle (N) (2) Repairs only

93) Removing / Repairing Flat Tire (E) (11) Major Roadway

96) Railroad Crossing (F) (5) Indicate feet from

97) Vacant Lot (G) (2)

98) Obstructing Driveway (F) (2)

09 Obstructing Traffic (E) (12)

Status Violation

72) Insp Stkr Mutilated / Counterfeit (NYS ONLY) (Specify) (J) (7)

73) Reg Stkr Mutilated / Counterfeit (NYS ONLY) Specify (J) (4)

75) No Match –Plates/ Sticker (J) (5)

83) Improper Registration (NYS ONLY) (J) (1)

Commercial Vehicle Violations

42) # Expired Muni – Meter Comm. Metered Zone (H) (10)

43) # Expired Meter. Comma Zone (H) (2)

44) @PKG in Excess of Posted Time Limits Comm Metered Zone (H) (5)

69) Failure to Display Muni Meter Receipt Metered Zone (H) (10)

47) Double PRK / Angle PKG – Midtown (Comm Vehicle) (I) (2) 14 St-60St
   1st Ave 8 Ave 7.am. -7P.M. except Sun

59) Angle PKG – Commercial Vehicles (K) (3) No Loading / Unloading or
   Obstructing. Traffic

82) Unaltered Commercial Vehicle (K) (1)

84) Platform Lifts in Lowered Position (Comm Vehicle Unattended) (K) (7)

85) @ Storage – 3 Hr. Commercial (K) (5)

86) @ Midtown PKG or STD – 3 Hour Limit (I) (3) 14 St - 60 St, 1 St – 8Ave
   7 A.M. – 7 P.M. Ex. Sun

Miscellaneous NYC traffic Rules and violations

79) @ Unauthorized Bus Layover (Section 4-10 (C) (3)

These are all the parking violation posted, more may come after this has been
posted.

State Codes

AL- Alabama

AK- Alaska

AZ- Arizona

CA- California

CO- Colorado

+Ct- Connecticut

DE- Delaware

+FL- Florida

GA- Georgia

HI- Hawaii

ID- Idaho

IL- Illinois

IN- Indiana

IA- Iowa

KA-Kansas

KY- Kentucky

LA-Louisiana

ME- Maine

+MD- Maryland

MA- Massachusetts

MI- Michigan

MN- Minnesota

MS- Mississippi

MO- Missouri

MT- Montana

NE- Nebraska

NV- Nevada

NH- New Hampshire

+NJ New Jersey

NM- New Mexico

+NY New York

+NC- North Carolina

OH- Ohio

Ok- Oklahoma

OR- Oregon

+PA- Pennsylvania

RI- Rhode Island

SC- South Carolina

SD- South Dakota

TN- Tennessee

TX- Texas

UT- Utah

VT- Vermont

+VT- Virginia

WA- Washington

DC- Washington, DC

WV- West Virginia

WI-Wisconsin

WY- Wyoming

Foreign Plates

AB- Alberta

BC- British Columbia

MB- Manitoba

NB- New Brunswick

NF- New Found land

NS- Nova Scotia

NT- Northwest Territories

NU- Nunavut

ON- Ontario

PE- Price Edward Island

QB- Quebec

SK- Saskatchewan

YT- Yukon

Diplomatic & Consulate Plates

GV- U.S. Government (Plate Type is always PSD)

DP- Diplomatic Plates (Plate Type is always PAS)

+ Common Codes: Fill-in oval provided on ticket

Plate Type Codes

AGR- Agriculture Vehicle

AMB- Ambulance

OMR- Bus

OMF- Bus Franchise

LMA- Class A Limited Use Motorcycle

LMB- Class B Limited Use Motorcycle

LMC- Class C Limited Use Motorcycle

PPH- Combat Wounded

CHC- Comm. Household

+ Comm- Commercial

CCK- County Clerk

DLR- Dealer

FAR- Farm Vehicle

FPW-Former Prisoner of War

HAM- Ham Operator

HR- Hearse Coach

HIS- Historical Vehicle

HOU- House/ Coach Vehicle

IRP- Intl.Registration Plan (Apportioned)

JCA- Justice Court Of Appeals

JCL- Justice Court Of Claims

SUP- Justice Supreme Court

OML- Livery

MED- Medical Doctor

MOT- Motorcycle

MCD- Motorcycle Dealer

NYA- N.Y. State Assembly

NYC- N.Y. Councilman

NYS- New York Senate

OMO- Omnibus – Taxi Service

ORG- Organization (PAS)

ORC- Organization (Com)

+ PAS- Passenger

PSD- Political Subd. (Official)

SPO- Pro Picture (Pas)

CSP- Pro Picture (Comm)

RGL- Regional

TRL- Regular Trailer

OMS- Rental

SCL- School Car

SEM- Semi- Trailer

+SRF- Special Registration Fee – Vanity

SRN- Special Registration No – Fee

SPC- Special Purpose Comm

STA- State Owned Vehicle

JSC- Supreme Court Appl. Div.

OMT- Taxi

TRC- Tractor

LTR- Trailer – Light

TRA- Transporter

USC- U.S. Congress

USS- U.S. Senate

OMV- Omnibus – Vanity

VAS- Voluntary Ambulance Service

WUG- World University Games

TMP- Temporary (NOT NY)

CMB- Combination (Connecticut)

HOLIDAYS

Any holiday that falls on the weekend will end of falling on the next business day depending on when that is.

New Year's Day - + always falls on Dec. 31 at midnight. Many people do volunteer to work on Jan.1 because the violation and the overtime are out there. **(MLH)**

(MLH) MEANS MAJOR LEGAL HOILDAY)

New Year's Day observed. (MLK)

Martin Luther King's Birthday, in Jan. **ASP.**

Asian Lunar New Year's, 1/23 **ASP.**

Lincolns Birthday, 2/12

Washington Birthday, Feb

Ash Wednesday, Feb

Purim, March

Holy Thursday, April.

Good Friday, April

Passover, April

Solemnity of the Ascension, April 29, 2015

Shavuot, May

Memorial Day, May

Independence Day (ALWAYS ON July 4)

Feast of the Assumption, Aug

Idul – Fitr, Aug

Labor Day, Sept

Rosh Hashanah, Sept

Yom Kippur, Sept

Succoth, (2 days) Oct

Columbus Day, Oct

Shemini Atzereth, Oct

Simchas Torah, Oct

Idul- Adha, Oct

All Saints Day, Nov

Election Day, Nov

Veterans Day, Nov

Divali, Nov

Thanksgiving Day, Nov

Immaculate Conception, Dec

Christmas Day, (Always on Dec 25)

Alternate Side Parking Rules Suspended (ASP)

"No Parking" signs in effect one day a week or on alternate days are suspended on days designated ASP; However, all "No Stopping "and "No Standing" signs remain in effect.

Major Legal Holiday Rules in Effect. (MLH)

"No Parking" and" No Standing" signs in effect fewer than 7 days a week are suspended on days designated MLH in the above calendar.

Parking Meter Zones

All "No Parking "signs in meter zones are suspended on ASP, Sunday and MLH days; however, meter must be activated during posted hours on ASP days.

Any holiday that is not posted, was not posted, when I posted them.

These days can vary according to your calendar. Even though these are all major holidays they are still in effect, meaning Traffic Agents will be working, as it stands Traffic Agents work 24 hours 7 days a week regardless of the holidays, they work, same as Police Department because this is the Police Department. Every command may not work 24/7 but each command does work every day. Nighthawks work overnights. Check out for the number so you can call them if needed. (718-385-0906) (Nighthawks)

On Snow Emergency days Traffic Agents are scheduled to work 7 x 7, meaning the A.M. tour will be working from 7 A.M. till 7 P.M. and the P.M. tours will be working 7 P.M. till 7 A.M. or basically till they get a one (1) on one (1) so they can leave, regardless who they maybe, which also includes Saturdays and Sundays. If they are working these days they are also working holidays as well. Nobody is permitted to work seven (7) days unless they want to, it's called voluntary overtime, nobody is permitted to work more than sixteen hours (16) in any day because that's the laws and if they try to work it, they can't although many Traffic Agents do push it and when they get into trouble for doing so, somebody has to explain it to the higher ups to check them or have someone else do what else were doing. Many Traffic Agents don't like to work and the ones that do or have keep doing them although like I said they can't work more than sixteen hours (16). All tow truck drivers are required to know what's done while working these tours. If anybody calls in sick leave it must be documented. All tow truck drivers with their tours would only be for days because if you're working, you're working.

I have also noticed that many people who were working with Traffic Agents, the Traffic Agents had to change their tours in order to work with other city agencies. This doesn't happen a lot or very often. Traffic Agents do try to work to pay off their bills like you and me.

The thing is that many Traffic Enforcement Agents do is try to do the work they were all hired to do, many people or Traffic Agents do is let their supervisors know there skills, computer skills is a must and if that Traffic Agents know the computer he is a she in, he can be in charge of others who don't a thing about the computers, others may have mechanical skills and can useful to his or hers supervisors.

I have also seen that many people who did work for Traffic Enforcement, many of them went to work for other Agencies, Commands, many of them went to become Police Officers, Corrections, or they went elsewhere because working within Traffic Enforcement stresses you to the point where you may get a heart attack or stroke or cardiac arrest, or worse, etc.

There are many different types of forms that the Police Department uses. Many of them are the ones (1) that I do know about. One (1) of them is the overtime form which is used daily, but not for everyone, number is PD 138-064, which you explain what's the overtime for and when did it happen. It can get to be complicated if it's not done right, and another form is used is for night shift differential form which is PD 433-041 which is used by all Traffic Agents for the hours of before 8 A.M. to 6 P.M. or after 6:00 P.M. for whoever works over these hours using.

It must be for over one (1) hour or else no night shift. Meaning if you worked till 6:30 P.M. and this is a part of your tour no nightshift differential will be given.

There are all kind of people out there and they are all different in different ways, we have Orientals, White, Jewish, Italian, Jamaican, Spanish, Puerto Ricans, Santa

Dominican, etc., all kinds of people and all of them want to learn how to get higher in life and to go as far as they can get.

When I said all kind of people all throughout this Department I meant it, there are all kind of people within this Department that are good at writing up Command Discipline, for the right things to where otherwise for a lot of nonsense which is no good, because if that particular person wants it he or she thinks that writing up everybody means your command need a lot of attention, when it don't.

Especially if you're a cadet in training getting a Command Discipline, then either he or she is in trouble for writing that Command Discipline without giving that Traffic Agent a chance to correct his or her problem because it escalates. Another thing is when you write all these command disciplines it does mean your command needs a lot of attention because really nobody wants to be writing up so many of these command disciplines, showing us all there is no problem within.

As I stated prior in the Police Department basically within Traffic Enforcement there are many different types of forms but the main forms that I did see alot of were overtime forms, nightshift differential forms, voidance forms, no hits, harms reports, incident reports, off duty employment forms, and a lot more that I can't remember right now or talk about.

Today I do see a lot of Traffic Agents as well Police Officers that do drive around in their cars or walking around mostly Traffic Enforcement Agents that are out of uniforms, meaning no hats or carrying them off their radio antennas, long sleeve shirts with their top buttons open, no ties around there necks or hanging off their shirts, or open shirts, no ties, walking or just too much jewelry around there necks to where it will take some time to get all that jewelry off so they just wear there long sleeve shirts with no tie. Driving cars I still see their drivers still park there department vehicles on a hydrants tagging other vehicles for whatever violations they may find instead of finding a legal parking spot so they can write legally.

Uniforms are not kept up to date by any means, many Traffic Agents and Police Officers don't wear there black straps with their black buckle, wear their shoes or actually sneakers because you can't shine the shoes they are presently wear by any means and nobody says or does anything about this. Some wear shoes that are just not the kind you're supposed to be wearing but again nobody says anything, maybe it's because maybe they are just comfortable, but you're still not permitted to be wearing them. Unless that may have changed.

As I said before I do see a lot of issues are not covered here but I'm trying to cover them the best way I remember.

Today and now it's almost the end of your tour which in the department eyes or rules is E.O.T, which means" End Of Tour" in the Police Department you are not permitted to just sign out not even if it's just tow two (2) minutes prior to the end of your tour because if you leave or even sign out you can be told no more because nobody within the Police Department is permitted to leave or it's called "Theft Of Services "which is also a Command Discipline. You signed in by the department clock hanging on by the front desk so you and they can see there correct time so must sign in, and sign out the correct time no matter what, that clock should be an electric clock, no batteries.

Today many Traffic Agents don't want to get this because if you're going to get that Command Discipline, it should be for something good, nothing bad. When I did write my Command Disciplines it was for something bad because that Traffic Agent caused did like lateness or worse insubordination or failing to follow orders.

But if you want you can leave by filling out a twenty eight (28) for that one (1) minute if you're allowed to. Usually it's a Police Departments higher rank or the I.C.O. who catches them, and it has been seen that everyone gets it because if one (1) Traffic Agent does it, then they all do it and the Traffic Supervisor takes the heat also for not watching there Traffic Agents who may leaving, although that particular Traffic Supervisor can't be in two (2) places at the same time, everyone wants to go home and nobody wants to hear anything you may have to say which does include the Police Department.

Today many people are trying to get into Traffic Enforcement just for the medical otherwise they are not into it at all and it can get very expensive. Today you must buy your own uniforms first, purchase them yourself which is a lot of money, you don't get uniform allowance till you've been on the job at least one(1) year, no absentees, for at least one(1) year, then you will be receiving your uniform allowance at Christmas time because that's when uniform allowance is. The tow uniform is altogether different because you're not really covered for that, your main uniform is the Traffic Enforcement Agents uniform, not the towing uniform, but if you do get into towing you must also buy that uniform and you keep all your uniforms up to date which is a lot of money.

As I try to finish it up I will say this, try to do your best work no matter who says differently, try. Nobody is perfect in anyway shape or form. I will say this, I did try to write this all up the best way I can considering my stroke and seizure it was really very hard to write. If you want this job, try to do it the best way you can, and be really careful doing it. Watch what goes on all around you because you are the ears and eyes all around. If you see something, say something.

ABOUT THE AUTHOR

I started my training writing summonses in August 2, 1982 and made supervisor in I believe April.1990. As a Supervisor I was located in the Manhattan Tow Pound because of my expertise in maintaining cars (linkages, opening car doors, etc). A friend of mine who is a Sergeant contacted me asked if I would be interested showing people where to find tows in the field. I contacted the Sergeant as requested and came up to the office to meet everyone. From that time, I opened up an exciting door to my future in this sector of the business world. I met a lot of people who were parts on the Police Department who found that I was very interested in towing, heavy duty trucks, buses, tractor trailers, detached trailers, if it was big enough to be towed, it was towed. I career ended on Jan 1014, then I was forced to RETIRE with a pipeline aneurysm, stroke & siezure.

Printed in the United States
By Bookmasters

This book is a collection of poems. In the poems' lines is describing some interesting moments of daily life about relationship between people, about beauty of nature, and about the different important events of social life. These poems are full of feelings, some of them full of love, some with feelings of disappointment about different problems, some of them with big moving and honor to some great people in our society. So many lines of these poems are full of passion for the beauty of nature of different cities and places. In the poems' lines like one of Perla's necklace are expressed diversity of feelings, like love, happiness, anger, hope, beauty, all those feelings that are campaigning everyone in daily life. This book is like one bouquet of "Poems of the Heart."

Durime P. Zherka (Bega) was born in Albania on March 17, 1956. She studied at the University of Agriculture Tirana, Albania, from 1975 to 1980. She graduated on June 30, 1980.

Durime came to the United States on August 26, 2000. Once in the United States, she studied at City College in Fort Lauderdale, Florida, from 2004 to 2006 and graduated as paralegal, associate degree, on March 30, 2006. She is studying project management, BA, at City College, Fort Lauderdale, Florida. She took citizenship on January 21, 2006.

authorHOUSE®

ISBN 978-1-5049-8346-4

51799

9 781504 983464